Freshwater Fishing

for Kids

Hunting and Fishing

Books for Kids

By

Isiah Maxwell

© Copyright 2018

All rights reserved.

Disclaimer Notice:

Please note the information contained within this document is for educational and entertainment purposes only. All effort has been executed to present accurate, up to date, and reliable, complete information. No warranties of any kind are declared or implied. Readers acknowledge that the author is not engaging in the rendering of legal, financial, medical or professional advice. The content within this book has been derived from various sources. Please consult a licensed professional before attempting any techniques outlined in this book.

By reading this document, the reader agrees that under no circumstances is the author responsible for any losses, direct or indirect, which are incurred as a result of the use of information contained within this document, including, but not limited to, — errors, omissions, or inaccuracies.

Table Of Contents

Introduction 7

Chapter One - Teach Fishing in Ten Steps........... 8

   Step 1: Find the Right Location.............................. 8

   Step 2: Organization is Essential 9

   Step 3: Safety First! 12

   Step 4: Discuss and Plan 13

   Step 5: Hold the Rod 14

   Step 6: Casting Technique..................................... 14

   Step 7: Gear 16

   Step 8: Live or Artificial Bait? 16

   Step 9: Land a Fish... 17

   Step 10: Have Fun 18

Chapter Two - Safety Tips 20

   Protective Eyewear... 20

   Barbless Hooks... 21

   PFD's 21

   Float and Line 21

Set Ground Rules 22

Nourishment 22

Kid-friendly Tackle.. 23

Fishing Gear 23

First-aid Kit 23

Whistle 24

Chapter Three - Fishing Poles and Lures 25

Hook and Worms 25

Best Fishing Poles for Kids.................................. 27

Starter Rod and Reel Combo................................ 27

Kid's Tackle Box 28

Bobbers.. 29

Soft Plastics 30

Landing Net... 30

Fishing Pliers...31

Fishing Gloves 31

Chapter Four - Basics of Fishing........................ 33

A Uni Knot.. 33

Running Sinker Rig 35

Set up Rod and Reel 35

Attach Bait 36

Attach Lure 37

Chapter Five - Create Young Conservationists .. 38

Conclusion 40

Resources 42

Introduction

In today's world, everything essentially depends on technology and if you are looking for an alternative way to organize a family activity, then fishing is a good option. It is useful because you will not only teach the child how to fish, but you will also teach the child to be patient, to think clearly, and to react immediately when the opportunity strikes. You can teach the child all this whilst having fun.

In this book, you will learn about the different steps you can follow to teach your child to fish, safety tips and the necessary tools to get started. If you are ready to learn about all this and more, then let us start without further ado!

Thank you once again for choosing this book. I sincerely hope you like it.

Chapter One - Teach Fishing in Ten Steps

Whenever you decide to teach a kid to fish, you need to keep a couple of things in mind. You need to ensure that the child is safe and that they experience their fishing experience in a stress-free environment. Follow the simple steps explained in this chapter to teach kids to fish. Once you check the last item off this list, you will know that you are ready to have some fun on the water and maybe even catch dinner!

Step 1: Find the Right Location

Remember, the primary objective of any fishing trip is to catch fish! Duh! So, if you want to avoid sad faces or a broken heart because you weren't able to catch any fish, then you need to make sure that you catch some fish. You need to find the right location. This is an essential step regardless of whether you want to sail on a boat or a kayak, or you plan to stay ashore or fish from a dock or not.

If you have a local fishing club, then you can ask them for advice. If not, you can always ask for advice at the local tackle shop. Also, you can ask for other information like suggestions for the best baits for a specific location, the kind of license you will need, and any other questions related to fishing regulations. If possible, then take the child along, as the child will also learn about the different aspects of this activity apart from catching fish.

Step 2: Organization is Essential

Once you start to prep for the fishing trip, you need to make a checklist. It will reduce the possibility of any last-minute stress and you will not have to worry about forgetting anything. So, check your list twice, when you pack your stuff and once before you head out. Here is a sample of a checklist that you can use before you head out on a fishing trip.

Like any outdoor activity, fishing requires specific gear like a fishing rod, tackle boxes, bait, hooks, lures, nets, and reels.

Snacks: you must never forget to carry snacks with you since you will be spending a lot of time on the open water. It is always a good idea to have a couple of snacks handy. You never know when the little ones might be hungry!

Drinks: carrying drinking water is quintessential to any fishing trip and you must not leave the house without a couple of bottles of drinking water at least. Being surrounded by water but being unable to consume it can be quite stressful. When you are out in the open for a long time, the elements of nature like the sun can cause dehydration. So, it is always a good idea to carry a couple of bottles of water. Apart from this, you can pretty much stock up on anything that you want to drink.

Sunscreen: fishing is an outdoor activity and you will spend a lot of time exposed to the sun. Even if it is not hot outside, spending a lot of time under the sun can cause sunburn. You must not only carry sunscreen with you, but you must also not forget to use it. Overexposure to the sun can cause troubles for not just adults, but children as well.

Bug repellant: if you are fishing in a pond, lake or a river, it means that there will be plenty of flies and other insects around you that can distract you. Bugs can also make your trip quite unpleasant. You can purchase bug repellant from a local tackle shop and hit the water only after you buy bug repellant. You will certainly be thankful for it later.

Rain jackets: getting caught in the rain is quite common. If you have been fishing for a while, then you might have experienced a sudden downpour at some point in time or other. You need to remember that no one can predict the weather accurately and you never know when it changes, so instead of risking the rain, it is better to carry a raincoat with you.

Hat: just like sunscreen, the hat will also protect your head from the sun rays. It also makes it easy to observe surroundings without the glare of the sun hitting your eyes.

Sunglasses: when the sun is shining high overhead, it can be difficult to see beneath the surface of the water due to the color difference. Sunglasses offer some shade and you will be able to see what is going on below the surface. Apart from this, sunglasses offer protection from the glaring sun rays and any potential damage to your eyes.

First-aid kit: regardless of how careful you are, accidents cannot be prevented. You must always carry a first-aid kit with you.

Ensure that you carry all these necessary items with you whenever you decide to go fishing. You are not only responsible for your safety, but you are responsible for the safety of the child present with you.

Step 3: Safety First!

If you don't pay attention to various aspects of safety when you have children around water, then it can prove to be quite a disaster. The first and foremost thing that you must always take is a life jacket. In case someone falls into the water, the life jacket will keep them afloat. Hooks are essential for fishing, but they can be quite problematic if you don't handle them properly. Hooks have barbs, so you need to be extra careful when you let children anywhere near sharp objects. You can always use something to hide the hook within the bobber so that it is safe for casting, especially for kids.

Step 4: Discuss and Plan

Children tend to be naturally curious regardless of their sex, age, geographic location and such. So, it is a good idea to explain certain things to them before you go fishing together. You can explain how a float works and how it tends to bob when the fish bites. If you start to cast, then tug on the line while making the kid hold the rod so that they know what a hit feels like. You need to show them how to set up the hook and all other aspects of fishing. It might take the child a while to understand all this, so make sure that you are patient with them.

Step 5: Hold the Rod

The first thing you must teach your child is to hold the rod properly. Remember to teach the child to always keep the rod in front of themselves, in a 9-11 o'clock position. Pay close attention to the way the child grips the rod. Carefully explain the way the reel handle works and the way to react when the fish bites. You must always be patient with children and don't be harsh. After all, you need to remember that they came on the fishing trip to learn.

Step 6: Casting Technique

There are two casting techniques; these techniques are the overhead cast and the sidearm cast. Usually, professionals and experienced fishermen tend to use the former and the latter is better suited for beginners.

Before you teach kids how to perform the sidearm cast, you need to make sure that no one is in the way. Take a look around to see if the coast is clear and then cast away! Now, you need to bring back the rod and make sure it stays above your waist while you are doing so. Swing the fishing rod forward while you flick your wrist and you release the line before the rod points towards the target. Once your rod points at the target, you need to stop.

It might take a child a couple of tries before he or she can do it well. In fact, it is quite likely that the first couple of attempts will not be a success. This is the time for you to maintain your calm and let the child practice some more. The more a child tries, the better the child will get at casting, so keep encouraging the child. You must never forget that you are dealing with a child and never lose your calm.

Step 7: Gear

I've already mentioned that you will need fishing gear. Up until now, you were learning about the steps to follow while teaching a child to fish. This information will not do you much good if you don't have the right gear for your fishing trip. You will need the right bobber, bait and a lightweight fishing rod. You also need some spin cast somewhere between 3'6" and 5' for successfully fishing. You will learn more about this in the coming chapters.

Step 8: Live or Artificial Bait?

To start with, it is always a good idea to start with artificial bait. It might scare the children if they need to use worms or minnows on their first fishing trip. Not only are artificial baits attractive and durable, they are easy to use as well. You merely need to rig them on a 1/32 to 1/8-ounce jig and it will do the trick for you. The best option for kids is bait is a jig dangled under a tiny float with an occasional twitch. It will show the kid how the bait behaves in water and you can show them how to reel and retrieve.

Step 9: Land a Fish

Catching fish certainly requires a lot of patience. You need to teach your young students to hold the rod steadily. You also need to show them to slowly reel the bait in when the fish reaches the surface. Also, you must show the child how this is to be done and don't do everything by yourself. If the child wants to try and land the fish by himself or herself, then you must let them. You can help them by giving the necessary instructions on how they need to react. Also, maintain a casual environment so that the child doesn't hesitate while asking for help. When the process is complete, and your child lands a fish, you can either release it or keep it for dinner! If you want to release the fish, then ask the child to not simply drop it or throw it back into the water. Instead, you need to show the child to slowly put it back and release it when the fish is completely submerged in water. If you want to use the fish for dinner, then you need to explain harvesting and why some fish need to be returned to the water.

Step 10: Have Fun

One thing you must not forget is that this is a fun activity, so you need to have fun and make sure that the children have fun as well. If you want the kids to come back with you on other fishing trips, the trip needs to be enjoyable and memorable. Don't worry about the numbers and instead concentrate on having fun. You might or might not catch anything, but the memories you make during this process matter the most. The biggest catch you can make is to get the child interested in fishing. Also, don't forget to bring a camera along with you to capture all the fun you had.

Follow the simple steps discussed in this chapter to teach your child how to fish and get started with fishing. The way you introduce fishing will make all the difference. So, make the activity fun and engaging and the child will certainly want more of it.

Chapter Two - Safety Tips

A family day spent on the water is a great way to have some wholesome fun together. There are a couple of safety tips that you need to keep in mind while fishing with kids. The joy of watching a child catch their first fish can be overshadowed by injury. So, as an adult, you need to ensure your child's safety before you do anything else. In this section, you will learn about the different safety tips you need to follow while fishing with kids.

Protective Eyewear

The first safety tip for fishing safely with kids is to use protective eyewear. To reduce strain on the eyes while spotting fish, use polarized sunglasses. Not just that, it will also offer protection from branches and lures while fishing. If you want to go fishing at night, you must also include a pair of clear glasses. You can buy clear glasses from a local hardware store.

Barbless Hooks

Always use barbless hooks because. They are easier to remove if a child or adult is snagged. These hooks are quite important when you are bait fishing and when you are using them, you need to slightly bend them down.

PFD's

PFD refers to a personal floatation device. Anyone can accidentally fall into the water, and to avoid accidents, always include a PFD in your fishing kit. A PFD is a must if you put the kids in a kayak, canoe, or a boat while fishing.

Float and Line

Regardless of whether you are fishing from the land or a boat, it is always good to have a float and line to toss to the kids in the water.

Set Ground Rules

You need to set some clearly defined rules and you need to make sure that the children follow these rules. Kids certainly love to have fun, but it is a recipe for disaster if they start running around a wet boat deck. You need to teach the child certain fishing skills as well as etiquette. You need to set some rules ahead of time and ensure that the children abide by them. This is incredibly important if you are fishing with a toddler. You are responsible for their safety and you need to teach the children about being safe while having fun. Also, setting certain rules reduces the risk of any accidents.

Nourishment

Never forget to carry drinks and snacks with you while going fishing. You will need sufficient snacks and water to prevent dehydration. Also, you never know when the child might be hungry! So, having a couple of snacks on hand is a good idea.

Kid-friendly Tackle

There are some rods that can be quite heavy, and a young child cannot handle these fishing rods well. The fishing equipment you use must be child-friendly. So, spend some time going through the list of ideal fishing gear and equipment given in this book.

Fishing Gear

Safety for kids while fishing also includes appropriate clothing. You always need to keep the kids warm and dry. So, you will need rain jackets or windcheaters, woolens to stay warm and a pair of boat shoes or sneakers to help with easy movement.

First-aid Kit

You need a first aid kit and; never do outdoor activities without carrying one with you. A typical first aid kit needs to include band-aids, bandages, gauze, disinfectant, pain medication, cotton, and allergy medication.

Whistle

Yeah, carrying a whistle might make you look like a coach or a lifeguard, but whenever the kids start to stray, a blast or two will certainly get them back.

If you keep all these things in mind, you will be able to handle almost any situation that comes your way and you can focus on fishing.

Chapter Three - Fishing Poles and Lures

Teaching a child to fish is a fun activity. Keep in mind that you are teaching a child to fish, so using a large or a heavy fishing pole will defeat the purpose. Children don't care if they are going to catch a five-pound bass or a three-inch bluegill. Children merely want to catch lots of fish. The idea is to bring them to a place where the fish will bite easily. In this section, you will learn about the different fishing poles and lures you can use to teach fishing.

Hook and Worms

You can use *Eagle Claw Snap*-on plastic bobber floats that are available in many sizes. These are great when you are teaching children to fish with small poles. The bobber is slightly heavy, and makes it easier to cast, and also allows you to cast the bait from the shore. Also, a large bobber gives the child a clear view of when the fish bite and the added weight keeps it submerged in water.

You can use an Eagle Claw Baitholder circle hook for a fishing pole. These hooks go perfectly well with bobbers. The barbs on this baitholder make it easier for the bait to hold on even when the fish start tugging on it. The circle hook needs to get caught in the fish's mouth. If you use J-hooks, make sure that you have no intention of releasing the fish back into the water. A J-hook is hard to remove because it gets hooked quite deep in a fish's stomach and can injure the fish severely.

You can use a treble hook since they also work really well with bobbers. These are the hooks that are used when fishing for trout. The three hooks present on the treble hook make it likely that at least one hook will catch the corner of a fish's mouth and the fish doesn't swallow it. It is also quite helpful when you want to hide small amounts of bait in the hook. If you want to a treble hook, then please consider the Gama katsu Treble Hook- sizes 14 to 18.

Best Fishing Poles for Kids

You not only need to use the right bait and lure but having the right size of pole also makes it easier for the kids to fish.

The *Shakespeare youth fishing pole* has a reel with a push button for toddlers. It is about two feet and six inches long and comes with a plastic practicing plug. This is suitable for children above the age of 4. It also comes in a different cartoon print. If your child is less than 5-years old, then you need to buy this fishing pole! You need to make sure that the child is holding on tightly to this pole. Since they are quite light, they can be tugged into the water when a big fish decides to bite.

Starter Rod and Reel Combo

Whenever you are selecting a fishing rod, you need to select one that is lightweight and is easy to use. It is always good to opt for a whirling pre-spooled rod and reel combo. The mechanism needs to be easy to use and simple to understand. Your little angler must be able to understand the basics of fishing without getting overwhelmed, or worse yet, frustrated!

The *Kid Casters Youth Fishing Kits* are a great option to start with. It comes with a 29.5-inch long fiberglass rod that is easy to use. The reel is also spooled with a 6-pound monofilament line, which is perfect for freshwater fishing. Remember, you need to keep your child's physical strength in mind when you select a fishing rod. After all, it is the child who needs to hold the rod and not you. Ideally, take the child along with you to the local tackle shop to select a reel and rod combo that works well for him or her. This fishing pole costs about $24 online.

Kid's Tackle Box

Every person interested in fishing needs a tackle box. When you are selecting a tackle box for a kid, you need something that is lightweight and secure.

It also needs to include a couple of beginner's tools and must provide sufficient space to include jigs, spinners, crankbaits, spoons, and plugs. The tackle box will essentially contain everything that a child will need to go fishing excluding the pole.

The Take Me Fishing tackle box is a good idea. It consists of a single tray box that is stocked with the bare essentials like hooks, sinkers, soft-body jigs, and bobbers. Also, the company that makes these tackle boxes donates a small portion of their proceeds to the Future Fisherman Foundation. You can buy this tackle box for $17.

Bobbers

When you are looking at bobbers, always opt for the Snap-On bobbers. These are easy to attach, and the kids don't need to tie them onto the line. Since you are just getting the children familiarized with fishing, it is always a good idea to start slow. Also, you are shopping for a child, so make sure that you select a bobber that is bright and colorful.

A fisherman needs to spend a major chunk of their time watching the bobbers, so you might as well make sure that the child has something good to look at. Also, a bobber gives the first indication when a fish tugs on the bait and it is quite engaging when the bobber has fun designs on it.

The TMNT rattle bobbers are easy to snap on and look like the ninja turtles.

Soft Plastics

These are great when you are introducing the child to lure fishing. They look quite natural and their wiggly nature helps attract fish. You need soft plastic with a single hook on the jig head. This is easier to handle than bait with trebles. You can change the lures you use according to the level of comfort of the child.

Landing Net

You need a landing net that is rubber coated so it

doesn't harm the scales of a fish and also reduces the chances of the fish getting stuck to the hook or getting tangled in the net. The Mad Bite's Foldable and Retractable Landing Nets are quite nice, so please do check them out before you buy a landing net. These nets have a hoop that's made of white e-glass that won't get dinged, unlike aluminum.

Fishing Pliers

You will need a pair of fishing pliers to not just secure the hooks and cut lines, but also to unhook catches. You need fishing pliers regardless of whether you are going bonefishing in the Bahamas or fishing for a crappie in Wisconsin. You need a pair of pliers that the child can hold onto easily and the jaws of the pliers need to be suitable for usage in fresh as well as seawater. The Bass Pro Shop's XPS Aluminum Pliers are worth buying.

Fishing Gloves

You need to buy your child a pair of fishing gloves

before you take them fishing. Look for a three-fingerless glove that frees up the thumb, middle finger and forefinger. These three fingers need to be unrestricted to improve the dexterity of the child casting the line.

Another item that you need to purchase is a life jacket or any other PFD. Find something that fits the child well and isn't too big or too small for the child.

Before you can take the children on a fishing trip, you need to make sure that they have all the necessary fishing equipment. You cannot teach anyone to fish without the necessary tools and the gear.

Chapter Four - Basics of Fishing

Dropping a line in the water might seem petty simple. To do this, you need a fishing rod, reel, bait, and some lures. If you are using bait, then you need to tie a simple rig of a little hook to a small sinker that helps to drop the bait into the water where the fish can bite.

A Uni Knot

If you don't know how to tie a basic knot, then you need to learn to tie fishing knots to attach the rigs and tie the hooks. The more you practice, the easier it becomes. In this section, you will learn about tying a simple uni knot that you can teach the kids when you take them fishing.

The uni knot is one of the most basic fishing knots and it is easy to learn. It is quite strong as well. Do you know how to tie shoelaces? If yes, then this is a very simple knot to master. There are four simple steps that you need to follow.

The first step is to take the hook and run a line through the eye of the hook and then double back to create a loop by letting the tag end over the double fishing line.

Now, you must wrap the tag end around the double line by going through the loop you created in the previous step.

You need to repeat this process six times to strengthen the knot.

Once you do this, you need to moisten the line and then pull the main line to tighten the knot.

If you aren't aware of what the tag end is, then it is the end of the line. You must always moisten the line to prevent any friction; it also prevents the knot from sliding along the line. You can wet the line by putting the knot in your mouth. You must also cut away any extra tagline that's there but never cut it too close to the knot. If you cut it too close to the knot, the knot will slide away.

Running Sinker Rig

You can use a running sinker rig to catch a wide array of fish in estuaries and even deep water. It is quite reliable and simple to make.

You need about a meter of the trace line or you can even use the main line if you don't have any trace line. Now, ask the child to tie a hook on one end and a swivel on the other end with the help of a uni knot.

Now, the child needs to thread a ball sinker through the main line and use a uni knot to join it to the other end of the swivel.

Set up Rod and Reel

You need to teach the child to set up the rod and the reel if you want to teach the child to fish. To set up the rod, the child needs to thread the line from the reel through the eyelets present on the rod and then pull it through so that a swivel, hook, or a clip can be attached to the end of the line. The hook and the sinker arrangement or anything else that you place at the end of the line is known as a rig. There are various types of rigs available and the one that you select will depend on the type of fish you want to catch and where you are fishing. You will need a small hook and sinker if you are taking your children fishing in calm water, whereas a big sinker and hook are essential if you are beach fishing.

Attach Bait

There are different types of baits you can use like squids, prawns, bread, and even worms. According to the species of fish you want to catch, the bait you use will differ. The size of the bait you use needs to be proportional to the hook you attach to the rod. If you want to catch small fish, then you need small pieces of bait and for a bigger species of fish, you need a larger hook or bait. While you are attaching bait to the hook, always ask the child to keep a portion of the barbed section of the hook exposed to increase the chances of catching fish.

Attach Lure

Lures are quite easy to store, and you can keep them in your tackle box. These come in handy especially when the fish are feeding close to the surface. Use lures when you notice fish close to the surface of the water. To attach a lure, ask the child to tie a small clip to the end of the trace line. Then the child merely needs to attach the lure to the clip. You can unclip the lure later if the fish don't bite.

Chapter Five - Create Young Conservationists

Rules of fishing might seem quite complicated to adults, let along children. You must never bombard children with a whole bunch of rules. Instead, explain in simple terms about things like licenses, size and gear restrictions. You need to teach children that poaching is frowned upon and that it is an illegal activity. Please tell that they can get into trouble if they don't follow fishing regulations, they can get into trouble.

Educate them about the fishing rules and tell them that those rules are in place to ensure that there is sufficient fish for everyone to catch. If a child wants to hold onto his or her catch, that's perfectly all right. If your child wants to eat his or her catch, then that is the right time to explain that you must only retain the catch that you want to eat and release the rest into the wild.

Fishing is an excellent means to teach children to

appreciate and respect nature. You can teach your child about the different parts of the fish anatomy while fishing. Water bodies are also home to several other creatures like minnows, macroinvertebrates and crawdads.

You must teach the child that fishing needs to be done in a sensible and responsible manner. Your acts must not disrupt the delicate balance of the ecosystem that we are a part of. Whenever you go fishing and you manage to catch a protected species, then you need to make sure that you immediately release it into the wild. You need to protect and respect nature.

Conclusion

Fishing is an activity that will provide you with not just memories but also with a perfect activity for bonding with children. Another wonderful aspect of fishing is that you have an opportunity to teach the kids about nature and how they need to respect it. Regardless of what you do, you must not force any activity on the child. If the kid asks you that he or she wants to leave, then it is time to head home. Don't exceed an hour or so on the first fishing trip. Once the child is big enough, you both will have a common activity to bond over.

Now, all that you need to do is take the first step and take your child on a fishing trip! Remember, safety first when it comes to any outdoor activity that involves your children. Thank you for your time and attention, and I wish you good luck fishing with your little one.

Finally, if you enjoyed this book then I'd like to ask you for a favor. Will you be kind enough to leave a review for this book on Amazon? It would be greatly appreciated!

Resources

https://www.takemefishing.org/how-to-fish/fishing-safety/fishing-with-kids/

https://www.globalfishingreports.com/kids-fishing-poles-and-lures/

CPSIA information can be obtained
at www.ICGtesting.com
Printed in the USA
BVHW040239021121
620536BV00018B/392

9 781790 905621